Get Tax Free Income from Municipal Bonds: High Yield Tax Exempt Interest

Fred Fuld III

DEDICATION

Dedicated to the investors who are looking for investments that can provide stable, steady income that is tax-free.

CONTENTS

INTRODUCTION

Investors looking for a place to park their money over the long term and achieve a high yield, should look no farther than municipal bonds, which generate tax free income.

Of course, you could leave your money in a savings account at a bank and receive one hundredths of one percent on your money, based on what banks are paying at that time this book was written. With the rates being paid on certificates of deposit, you can boost your yield to 0.17% on a CD.

Or you could invest in high yield dividend paying stocks, and subject yourself to the volatility of the stock prices and the taxes on the dividends.

So municipal bonds may be the way to go. This book will cover the basics of municipal bonds, the advantages and disadvantages of munis, and why you might or might not consider municipal bond closed end funds or muni mutual funds.

1 WHAT IS A MUNICIPAL BOND

High income taxpayers love municipal bonds, as they provide income that is tax free from Federal income taxes, and if the bond is issued from the state in which the taxpayer resides, with a few exceptions, interest is exempt from state income taxes. If you own a bond from one of the territories and possessions of the US such as Puerto Rico, Guam, the Virgin Islands, American Samoa, the Northern Mariana Islands, or the District of Columbia, then the income is generally exempt from state income taxes also.

Municipal bonds are issued by states, counties, cities, and other governmental entities such as school districts, sewer districts, bridge authorities, and water and power departments.

So let's start with the real basics. What is a bond? A bond is a loan from an investor to a corporation or a governmental entity. For purposes of this discussion, the governmental entity agrees to pay back the amount borrowed on a specific date, called the maturity date, and in the mean time, pay the investor a specific amount of interest, with payments make on a semi-annual basis.

A municipal bond is sometimes referred to as a tax free bond or a tax exempt bond or a muni for short.

Since the municipal bonds are only paid twice a year, some investors choose bonds with varying interest payouts:

January – July

February – August

March – September

etc.

so that income is coming in every month.

The maturity date allows investors to plan ahead, and make a determination about whether they are going to use the proceeds for a specific purchase, or roll the money over to more bonds.

Bonds are generally divided into two different categories: general obligation bonds and revenue bonds.

General obligation bonds are backed by what is referred to at the "full faith and credit' of the issuing government. What that means, in essence, it is based on the taxing ability of the governmental entity.

Revenue bonds are backed solely and exclusively from the revenues generated by the operations of the entity, such as bridge tolls, government owned airport revenues, toll road tolls, water district revenues, and so forth.

Some investors consider general obligation bonds to be the safer of the two, because of the ability to tax and raise taxes. But as we have seen in the past, some governments have gone bankrupt. Look what happened to Detroit, Michigan in 2013 and Stockton, California in 2012.

Detroit Bankruptcy Filing

However, other investors feel that the revenue bonds are safer, as the revenues will always be coming in to pay the interest on the bonds. And as long as the debt coverage is good, the bond should be safe. The debt coverage refers to the amount of revenues coming in versus the interest being paid out.

2 A LITTLE HISTORY

The first American municipal bond was issued by New York City in 1812, to build a canal. It was a general obligation bond, backed by the taxing authority of the city. As the mid-century approached, the number of municipal bonds issued by cities began to expand tremendously.

It wasn't just the East Coast governments that were issuing munis; western cities, such as San Francisco, started issuing them also. As a matter of fact, the following bond from the City and County of San Francisco was issued on April Fools Day in 1866.

San Francisco Municipal Bond

During the 1873 crash, the issuance of municipal bonds came to a standstill. But after several years, municipals were on the rise again.

Originally, munis were issued as paper documents, with one page for the bond and attached pages of coupons. Each coupon represented one interest payment. The bond holder would cut off the coupon when the date arrived that matched the date on the coupon, take the coupon to their bank, and either cash it or deposit it in a bank account. In other words, the coupons were like cash.

Municipal Bond from Cerritos, California

These bonds were what are referred to as bearer bonds. This means that whoever holds the bonds, owns the bonds. So it wasn't just the coupons that were like cash, it was the whole bond that was like cash. If you lost the bond, if it was stolen, or burned in a fire, you were out of luck.

Some "dishonest" investors would get around the estate tax for their heirs by keeping the bonds in an accessible place that the heirs could get to upon death. Then the heirs wouldn't report the bonds as part of the estate.

Partly for this reason, and partly for the risk of loss, municipalities were encouraged to issue their bonds as registered bonds, which means that the name of the owner was typed on the bond.

Eventually, with the advent of technology, investors were given the choice of having the bond registered or holding it in street name, whereby the brokerage firm would hold on to the bond and the investor would just receive a monthly statement showing the bond holdings.

Now the munis are issued electronically. Investors can check their bond holdings online, and receive statements, either electronic or paper, periodically from the broker.

Currently, the interest payments on munis are credited to your brokerage account, automatically deposited in a bank account, or for the investors that still likes low tech, have a check sent out.

It is a big change from the old days of clipping the coupons.

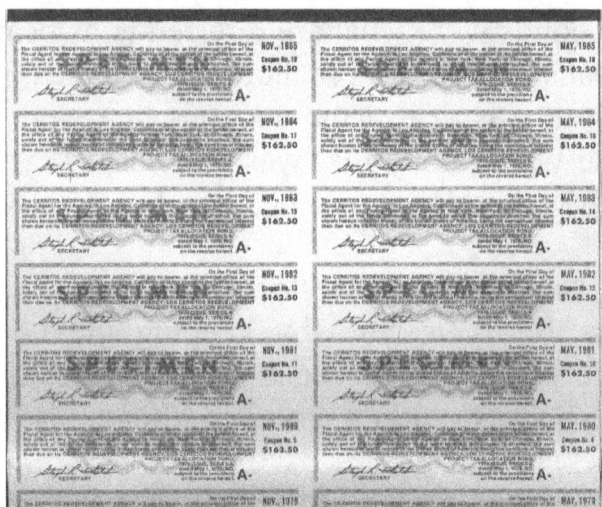

Municipal Bond Coupons

By the way, here's a bit of trivia. Years ago, wealthy men and women were often referred to as "coupon clippers." The phrase came about because the wealthy owned municipal bonds and they would get their interest by clipping the coupons off of their municipal bond coupon sheets.

3 RATINGS AND DEFAULTS

There are three major credit rating agencies that rate municipal bonds. They are:

Standard & Poor's
Moody's
Fitch Ratings

Bonds are rated using a letter ranking designation. Moody's used Aaa, Aa, A, and Baa for investment grade bonds, which used to be referred to as "bank quality bonds" as banks could only buy bonds with one of the four highest rankings. The designations of Ba, B, Caa, Ca, and C are used for lower quality bonds with a higher risk of default.

S&P and Fitch utilize AAA, AA, A, and BBB for investment grade bonds with BB, CCC, CC, C, and D for the lower quality.

The amount of default for investment grade bonds is far lower than the defaults on corporate bonds with similar ratings.

As a matter of fact, using the Moody's rating as an example, for bonds with an investment grade, the number of municipal defaults was only seven one hundredths of a percent (0.07%), versus corporate bonds of the same investment grade which had defaults amounting to in excess of two percent (2.09%). This is based on the following analysis from the House Report 110-835 of the U. S. Government.

CUMULATIVE HISTORIC DEFAULT RATES
[In percentages]

Rating categories	Moody's		S&P	
	Muni	Corp	Muni	Corp
Aaa/AAA....................	0.00	0.52	0.00	0.60
Aa/AA.....................	0.06	0.52	0.00	1.50
A/A........................	0.03	1.29	0.23	2.91
Baa/BBB...................	0.13	4.64	0.32	10.29
Ba/BB.....................	2.65	19.12	1.74	29.93
B/B........................	11.86	43.34	8.48	53.72
Caa-C/CCC-C...............	16.58	69.18	44.81	69.19
Investment Grade..........	0.07	2.09	0.20	4.14
Non-Invest Grade..........	4.29	31.37	7.37	42.35
All.......................	0.10	9.70	0.29	12.98

Source. Moody's, S&P, via the U. S. Government GPO.
[House Report 110-835]
[From the U.S. Government Printing Office]

4 BUYING ALTERNATIVES

When you buy municipal bonds, you should be aware of the minimum requirements of the brokerage firms that you buy your bond through. Many have minimums of $10,000 to $15,000 per transaction, and some have a minimum of $25,000. This is in spite of the fact that municipal bonds are issued in $5,000 denominations.

If you don't want to put that much into one bond, you have some options. You can buy municipal bond mutual funds and municipal bond closed end funds.

The tax free mutual funds generally have minimums of $1,000 to $2,500. A couple of the mutual fund families that have offered minimums as low as $100, such as Dupree Mutual Funds. You would need to check their current prospectuses to confirm that the low minimums are still in place.

The minimum for closed end funds, which are commonly referred to as CEFs, have an even lower minimum. You could theoretically buy one share of a CEF. There are over 100 of these municipal bond CEFs that pay out tax free income.

There are many advantages to owning CEFs besides

the fact that there is no minimum investment, but there are also some big disadvantages. These advantages and disadvantages will be covered in later chapters in this book.

Of course, many years ago, the minimum purchase amount wasn't an issue. As an example, some municipal bonds were issued in denominations of only five dollars per bond, such as bonds issued by the State of Louisiana.

Louisiana $5 Baby Bond with four coupons

5 THE TAX EXEMPT INCOME BENEFIT

The biggest benefit of munis that attracts investors is the fact that the bonds pay tax-free interest. From a Federal tax standpoint, the interest is exempt from income taxes. On the state side, it is a little bit tricky, because it depends on the state that you live in.

In general, if the bond was issued in the state you live in, the interest is exempt from state income taxes. This especially applies to the larger states, such as California, Massachusetts, Michigan, New Jersey, New York, Pennsylvania, and many other states.

Of course, there are a few states that don't have a state income tax, so this wouldn't be an issue for the residents of such states as Alaska, Florida, Nevada, Texas, and a few others.

However, if you live in Illinois, Iowa, Oklahoma, Utah, or Wisconsin, you need to check with your accountant and your bond broker regarding the taxation of muni bond interest from bonds issued in those states, as it could even depend on the specific bond.

So let's say you live in California, Michigan, or New York, as an example, and you own a lot of bonds from your own state, you want additional diversification, but you also still want interest exemption from state income tax. Where can you invest?

If you are willing to accept the risks, you can consider investing in bonds issued by one of the territories and possessions of the United States. These include Puerto Rico, Guam, the Virgin Islands, American Samoa, and the Northern Mariana Islands. American who own bonds from these territories receive interest that is tax free from both state and Federal income tax. This is due to Federal Law.

As an example, for Puerto Rico, according to 48 U.S. Code § 745:

All bonds issued by the Government of Puerto Rico, or by its authority, shall be exempt from taxation by the Government of the United States, or by the Government of Puerto Rico or of any political or municipal subdivision thereof, or by any State, Territory, or possession, or by any county, municipality, or other municipal subdivision of any State, Territory, or possession of the United States, or by the District of Columbia.

Historically, these territory bonds have been issued ratings that are on average lower than the ratings of state issued bonds, but they still usually carry bank quality bond ratings.

Another alternative is by purchasing bonds issued by the District of Columbia. Interest on those bonds is also exempt for all U.S. residents.

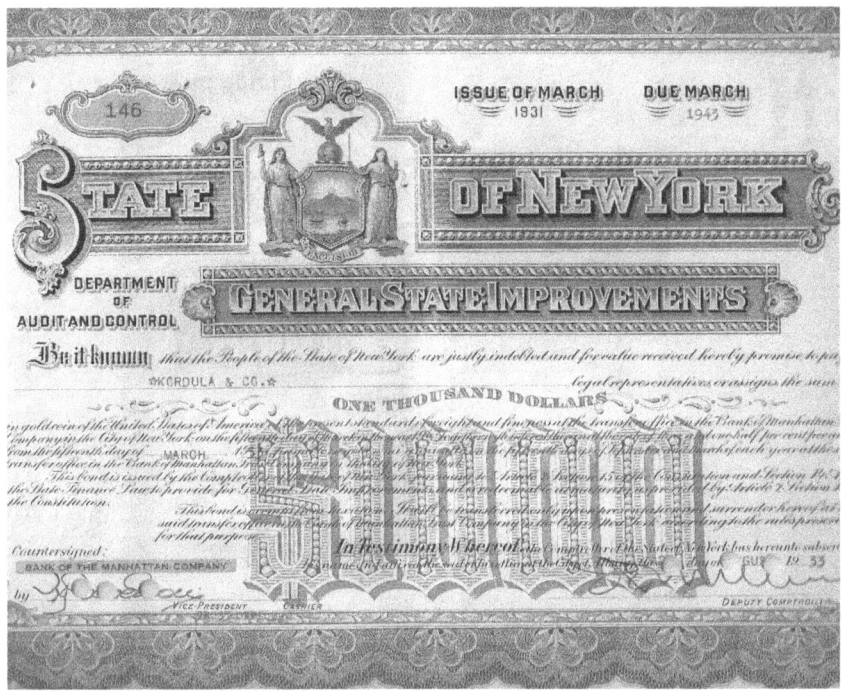

New York City residents may get a triple tax exemption. Interest on munis from the state of New York are exempt from city and state income taxes, along with Federal taxes.

There are certain municipal bonds called private activity bonds. These are bonds issued to fund hospitals, housing projects, stadiums, airports, and other entities. These bonds may trigger the alternative minimum tax.

One tax issue you should be aware of is that the municipal bond interest can affect the taxation of Social Security income. Talk to your accountant about this if you are receiving Social Security benefits.

6 ADVANTAGES OF MUNIS OVER CEFS

Individual municipal bonds have several advantages over municipal bond closed end funds. You can pick and choose what governmental agency you want to loan money to. Maybe you want to stick with the bonds from the cities and counties near you that you are familiar with.

Bonds have a maturity date. This is probably the most important benefit of buying individual bonds over the CEFs. The reason why this is so significant is that no matter how high interest rates go, and no matter how low the bonds drop in value, at maturity, the bonds are paid off at par.

What your bond is trading at is what your bond is worth; in other words, the trading price of CEFs may be trading at a far higher or lower price than the net asset value of the fund.

No Taxes on High Yield Interest

7 DISADVANTAGES OF MUNIS VERSUS CEFS

One of the biggest disadvantages of individual municipal bonds is the higher minimum investment. Although munis are issued in $5,000 denominations, the minimum as many firms have a minimum purchase of $10,000 to $25,000. A round lot is often considered by some firms to be $100,000.

There is also less diversification when you invest in individual bonds. Because of the higher minimum, investors can't own as many diverse bonds as they could with a CEF. Let's assume you have $25,000 to invest in tax free bonds. If you buy individual bonds, you will be lucky to buy more than a couple issues, versus a CEF which could have dozens of the bonds in its portfolio.

Interest payments on munis are paid only twice a year. Without a lot of bonds with varying maturity months, the interest would come in with peaks and valleys.

There is no professional management or monitoring. You would have to be your own manager, and do your own monitoring.

There is a lack of liquidity. Munis are not traded on an exchange, and estimated prices given on brokerage statements can be way off from what brokers will actually offer you if you want to sell. This actually happened to me; I received an offer of five points less (5% less) than what the statement showed a couple days before, with no change in interest rates over those couple days. So you are at the mercy of what the broker offers.

8 ADVANTAGES OF CEFS OVER MUNIS

The advantages of buying municipal bonds are varied. First, there is no minimum investment. You could technically buy one share of the CEF.

Second, the investor can receive monthly income. If you want income coming in every month, CEFs can provide that as most pay dividends monthly.

Plus, the monthly income can be reinvested. With the monthly income, you receive your capital back faster, and you can achieve quicker compounding of your income.

CEFs are very liquid; they are traded on major exchanges including the New York Stock Exchange and NASDAQ. You can track the CEF prices on the Internet. Whereas, when you try to sell a municipal bond, you call a broker, they try to get a bid, and get back to you later in the day or the following day with a bid.

The bid and asked spreads on CEFs are very narrow compared to municipal bonds. The bid price is what you can sell at and the asked price is what you can buy at. The spread is the difference between the two prices.

If you need some funds from your investment, you can

sell off small portions of the CEF holdings if money is needed. In other words, if you had $10,000 invested and needed to cash in $1,000 worth, you could do it with a CEF by selling off enough shares, but you could not do that with municipal bonds.

9 DISADVANTAGES OF CEFS VERSUS MUNIS

Now for the disadvantages of CEFs. First, there is a management fee and other administrative fees on the funds.

Some CEFs use leverage in order to boost their yields. You should beware that this increases the risks to the investor.

Some CEFs may be trading at a premium to net asset value. The net asset value is what the investors would get for each share if the CEF sold off all bonds and distributed the proceeds among all the shareholders on a per share basis. If you decide to buy a CEF, you should look for those trading at a discount.

There is no maturity date on CEFs (with the exception of a few target funds). If rates go up and continue to rise during your lifetime, you may never get your principal back.

10 PRICING OF BONDS

A bond that is selling for its face value is selling at par. The pricing on a bond selling at par is 100. The 100 represents the percentage of face value. However, if the bond is trading at 95, you don't say the price is 95%, you say the price is 95.

A $5,000 bond trading at 95 would be selling at $4,750, which is 95% of $5,000. A bond could also be selling at 103, which for a $5,000 bond would be $5,150.

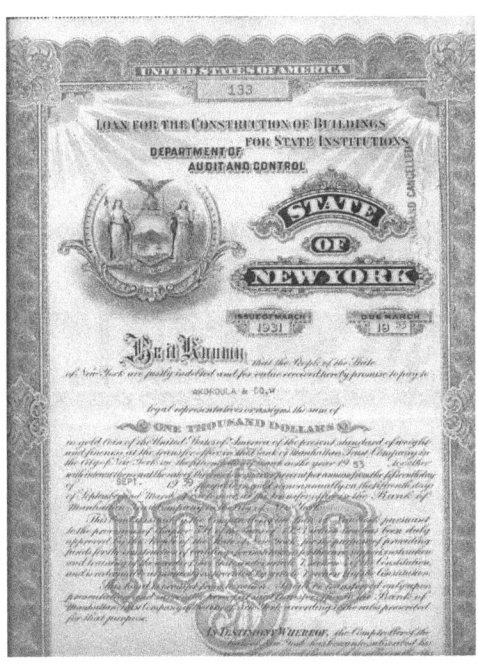

11 BOND YIELDS

There are three primary yields that you should be aware of for municipal bonds:

Coupon Rate

Current Yield

Yield to Maturity

The coupon rate, is the rate that the bond is paying upon its initial issuance. In other words, if a $5,000 bond was originally issued at 4%, the 4% is the coupon rate, and therefore pays $200 per year.

The current yield is calculated by taking the annual income that the bond pays and dividing it by the current price of the bond.

For example, if the same $5,000 bond with a 4% coupon is selling for 96 or $4,800, the current yield would be 4.17%. If the bond is selling for 104 or $5,200, the current yield would be 3.85%.

The yield to maturity (YTM) is determined using a very complicated formula that requires a bond calculator or an advanced spreadsheet function (YIELDMAT on Excel). Of course, the bond brokers will publish the yield to maturity on their list of bonds in inventory that are available for sale on their web site.

The yield to maturity takes into consideration the premium or discount on the bond. For example, a $5,000 bond with a coupon of 4.125% that matures in 16 years selling for 103, has a yield to maturity of 3.87% versus a current yield of 4.00%.

One other yield that you should be aware of is the yield to first call. A call is a feature written into the bond agreement, known as an indenture, that says the governmental entity can buy the bond back at par or at a premium earlier than the maturity date. Borrowers may do this because they can refinance the existing bonds at a lower interest rate or have accumulated excess cash.

Investors pay close attention to the yield to first call, because it can be lower than the yield to maturity. Also, if the bond is called, interest rates may be much lower and you would not only lose the high income on the current bond, but you would have to reinvest the called funds at a much lower interest rate.

12 HOW TO PURCHASE MUNICIPAL BONDS

There are many places to buy municipal bonds. The first step is opening an account. If you have opened a stock brokerage account, it would be very similar if not identical.

You have the option of buying from a major brokerage firm that offers all types of investments, not just munis, or from a company that specializes in municipal bonds.

The easiest and simplest way is to check out the web sites of some of the various firms. Find out what their minimum investment is, and check out the bonds they have in inventory.

Here are some brokers that sell municipal bonds in no particular order. I have dealt with several of them and had a great experience with them, but I am not making recommendations for any of them. I am also not compensated for providing information on these companies. I just want to give you some choices to pick from.

Alamo Capital
alamocapital.com

FMS Bonds Inc.
fmsbonds.com

Merrill Edge (Merrill Lynch/Bank of America)
merrilledge.com

TDAmeritrade
tdameritrade.com

Wulff, Hansen & Co.
wulffhansen.com

Hennion & Walsh
hennionandwalsh.com

13 ZERO COUPONS BONDS

Zero coupon bonds are bonds that don't pay any current income, but are issued at a huge discount to par, and the return comes from receiving the face value at maturity.

Often these are bought when a specific amount of money is needed at a specific time, with a smaller amount of money that is currently available.

For example, a zero coupon bond selling at 28.55 (28.55% of face value) that matures in 27.5 years, has no coupon yield, no current yield, but a yield to maturity of 4.62%.

So using this same example, if you were retiring in twenty seven and a half years, and you wanted to have $100,000 in a particular investment at that time, you would only need to put up $28,550 now, and not pay any tax on the bonds during your holding period, and not pay any tax at maturity.

14 PRE-REFUNDED BONDS

Pre-Refunded Bonds are municipal bonds which have been refinanced, the proceeds of the refinance being held in escrow in U.S. government securities, until the call date on the bonds.

Often, municipal bonds are issued in a high interest rate environment. When interest rates drop, governmental entities with these high interest bonds outstanding can issue newer bonds at lower interest rates, the proceeds of which can be used to pay off the higher rate bonds.

However, the higher rate bonds usually have a first call date that is several years in the future. So the proceeds from the lower interest bonds are held in escrow, with the assets generally invested in U.S. government securities, until the call date on the high interest bonds. At that time, the higher interest rate bonds are paid off.

Because of the fact that the pre-refunded bonds are essentially paid off, are backed by U. S. government securities, and are guaranteed to be paid off at the upcoming call date, they are considered extremely safe, and probably the safest of all municipal bonds.

15 ESCROWED-TO-MATURITY BONDS

Escrowed-to-maturity bonds, also referred to as ETM bonds, are bonds that have been pre-refunded with enough funds to cover principal and interest until maturity.

These bonds are similar to the Pre-Refunded Bonds (see previous chapter), with which the proceeds of the refunding are held in escrow in safe treasury securities.

However, they are designed to be paid of at maturity instead of the first call date, yet some issuers reserve the right to use the funds to pay off early at first call instead of at maturity.

No Taxes on High Yield Interest

16 INSURED MUNICIPAL BONDS

Insured municipal bonds are bonds that have their principal and interest insured by a private insurance company. Often, issuers pay for insurance on their bonds in order to induce investors to buy their bonds, and to provide an additional level of security and comfort to investors.

In addition, and more importantly, insured municipal bonds have carried a lower interest rate than non-insured bonds, saving issuers significant amounts of money in interest over the life of the bonds.

The major insurers of municipal bonds are:

• Municipal Bond Insurance Association (MBIA)

• American Municipal Bond Assurance Corporation (AMBAC)

• Financial Guaranty Insurance Company (FGIC)

17 ORIGINAL ISSUE DISCOUNT BONDS

Original-issue discount bonds are municipal bonds that were issued on their original offering below face value. This gives the bonds a special Federal tax benefit, whereby the difference between the price that the bond was issued at and the face value at maturity is considered tax-exempt income as opposed to capital gains, when the bonds are held to maturity.

If they are sold prior to maturity, talk to your accountant about the tax ramifications of the gain upon sale.

18 CONDUIT BONDS

Municipal borrowers sometimes issue bonds on behalf of private entities such as non-profit colleges or hospitals. These "conduit" borrowers typically agree to repay the issuer, who pays the interest and principal on the bonds. These are referred to as Conduit Bonds.

In cases where the conduit borrower fails to make a payment, the issuer usually is not required to pay the bondholders.

No Taxes on High Yield Interest

19 THE RISKS

There are risks with investing in municipal bonds as there is with all investments. Here is a list of the primary risks involved.

Interest rate risk

Bonds have a face value, which is called the par value. At maturity, the investor receives the face value amount, along with interest. The market price of the bond will move up when interest rates decline and it will drop as interest rates go up, so the trading price of the bond may be more or less than the face value. Interest rates in the U.S. have been low for quite a while. If interest rates move higher, investors with a low fixed rate municipal bond who want try to sell it before by maturity may lose money because of the lower price of the bond.

Credit risk

Credit risk is the risk that the issuer might incur financial problems that would preclude it from paying interest and principal, in which case, the issuer would be in default. Fortunately, a large number of bonds have credit ratings which approximate the relative credit risk of a bond compared to other bonds. However, even though a bond may have a high rating, it could still default.

Call risk

Call risk is the possibility of an issuer to repay a bond before its maturity date, which is something that the issuer would probably do if interest rates drop. When interest rates are stable or moving higher, bond calls rarely happen. Since so many municipal bonds are callable, investors should be aware of the call date if they plan on holding the municipal bond to maturity.

Inflation risk

Inflation is a general rise in prices, in very simple terms. Inflation reduces purchasing power of consumers, which is a type of risk for investors that have a bond with a fixed rate of interest. Inflation also can lead to higher interest rates which would cause a lower market value for existing bonds.

Liquidity risk

Liquidity risk is the risk that investors will have a limited market for the municipal bond, which could prevent them from selling the bond when desired and getting a reasonable price for the bond. Most investors acquire municipal bonds to hold them to maturity, so the market for a certain bond may not be liquid.

20 FACTORS TO CONSIDER BEFORE INVESTING

You should consult an accountant or other tax professional to determine the bond's tax implications, especially considering the chance that your bond may be subject to the Federal alternative minimum tax. Plus, you can find out about the state income tax benefits of the bond.

Municipal bond brokers are paid from a markup over the cost of the bond to the brokerage firm. The markup is generally not disclosed on your confirmation statement. However, if a separate commission is charged, it would be shown on the confirmation statement. Ask your broker about markups and commissions before making a purchase.

Checkout the background of the broker offering the bond to you. A seller of securities must be licensed, and the salesperson's firm must be registered with one or more of the following: the MSRB (Municipal Securities Rulemaking Board), FINRA (Financial Industry Regulatory Authority), the SEC (Securities & Exchange Commission), and a state securities department.

Investors can check out an investment adviser on the SEC's Investment Adviser Public Disclosure website at:

www.adviserinfo.sec.gov

Check out brokers on FINRA's BrokerCheck website at:
www.finra.org/brokercheck

To confirm MSRB registration, you can review the MSRB's registered dealers list at:
http://www.msrb.org/msrb1/pqweb/registrants.asp

21 FINDING MORE INFO ON MUNICIPAL BONDS

Investors desiring more information on municipal bonds can check out a wide range of resources online at no cost, at the Municipal Securities Rulemaking Board's Electronic Municipal Market Access (EMMA) website.

This information includes disclosure documents going back as early as 1990, which includes a bond's official statement. The official statement is a disclosure document similar to a prospectus that contains important information, such as maturity, type, yield, credit quality, call features and risk factors, plus audited financial statements, material events, ratings changes, any payment delinquencies and any defaults.

EMMA also provides historical and real-time transaction price data, including data relating to variable rate demand obligation bonds, which resets its interest rate at regular intervals. For bonds that don't trade very often, recent price information may not be available.

22 SUMMARY

Municipal bonds, which are often referred to as munis, are debt investments issued by states, counties, cities, and other governmental entities to finance day-to-day obligations and to pay for capital projects such as building highways, hospitals, schools, or sewer systems.

A purchaser of municipal bonds is lending money to the bond issuer in exchange for an agreement of regular interest payments, almost always semi-annually, and the return of the original investment at a particular point in the future.

A municipal bond's maturity date is the date when the issuer of the bond pays back the principal. It could be one year or many years in the future. Short-term bonds mature in one to three years and are usually referred to as notes, while long-term bonds have much longer maturity dates.

Usually the interest on municipal bonds is exempt from federal income tax, and may also be exempt from state and local taxes if you live in the state where the bond is issued. Bond investors usually look for a steady stream of income payments and may be more risk-averse and more focused on preserving capital, as opposed to capital gains. Because of the tax benefits, the interest rates on municipal bonds are generally lower than on taxable corporate bonds.

The two most common types of municipal bonds are general obligation bonds and revenue bonds.

General obligation bonds are issued by states, cities or counties and not backed by any specific assets. However, general obligation bonds are backed by the full faith and credit of the issuer, which can tax its citizens to cover payments on the bonds.

Revenue bonds don't have the backing of the government's taxing power. Revenues are generated from a specific project, such as bridge tolls or highway tolls. Investors should be aware that some revenue bonds are non-recourse, meaning that if the revenue stream goes away, the bondholders would not have a claim on the underlying revenue asset.

23 ONLINE RESOURCES

Municipal Securities Rulemaking Board
Electronic Municipal Market Access (EMMA)
http://emma.msrb.org/Home

Municipal Securities Rulemaking Board's Education Center
https://www.msrb.org/EducationCenter.aspx

SEC's Investment Adviser Public Disclosure
http://www.adviserinfo.sec.gov

FINRA's BrokerCheck
http://www.finra.org/brokercheck

MSRB's registered dealers list
https://www.msrb.org/regulated-entities/registration-status

FINRA: Municipal Bonds—Important Considerations for Individual Investors
http://www.finra.org/investors/alerts/municipal-bonds_important-considerations-individual-investors

SEC's Office of Municipal Securities
http://www.sec.gov/municipal

Municipal Securities Rulemaking Board EMMA Education Center
http://emma.msrb.org/EmmaHelp/EmmaHelp.aspx

Municipal Securities Rulemaking Board
http://www.msrb.org

Bloomberg Municipal Repository
http://www.bloomberg.com/markets/rates-bonds/government-bonds/us

DPC Data
http://www.munifilings.com/munifilings/IndexAction.do

Interactive Data Pricing and Reference Data
https://www.theice.com/solutions/data

Standard & Poor's
http://www.standardandpoors.com/home/en/us

FINRA's Market Data Center
http://www.finra.org/marketdata

Wall Street News Network
http://WallStreetNewsNetwork.com

SEC's Frequently Asked Questions
https://www.sec.gov/answers/faqs.htm

NASAA

North American Securities Administrators Association

This is the organization that provides resources and contact information for state and provincial securities regulators for all U.S. states, U.S. Territories, and Canadian provinces.

https://www.nasaa.org/contact-your-regulator/

GLOSSARY

Alternative Minimum Tax -– Tax on an adjusted amount of taxable income above a certain threshold

AMBAC - American Municipal Bond Assurance Corporation

American Municipal Bond Assurance Corporation – One of the major insurers of municipal bonds

AMT – Alternative Minimum Tax

Basis point -– one hundredth of a percent

CD – Certificate of deposit

CEF – Closed End Fund

Closed End Fund – An Investment company with a fixed number of shares that owns a diversified group of stocks or bonds, and trades on an exchange, with trade prices that could be above or below the net asset value

Coupon – A small certificate representing a six month

interest payment on a bond

Coupon rate – The interest rate on a bond at issuance

Current yield –The yield calculated by dividing the annual interest payment on a bond divided by the current price of a bond.

Discount – A bond selling at a discount is selling below par or face value

Face value – The amount that the bond was originally issued for and what will be paid at maturity. Modern bonds generally have a minimum face value of $5,000

FGIC - Financial Guaranty Insurance Company

Financial Guaranty Insurance Company - One of the major insurers of municipal bonds

Fitch – A municipal bond rating agency

Indenture – A legal document (printed on the face of the bond for bonds issued in paper format) that specifies the obligation of the borrower

Insured municipal bond – A bond that has its principal and interest insured by a private insurance company

MBIA - Municipal Bond Insurance Association

Moody's – A municipal bond rating agency that also rates other investments

Municipal Bond Insurance Association - One of the major insurers of municipal bonds

Municipal bonds - Bonds issued by states, counties, cities, and other governmental entities such as school districts, sewer districts, bridge authorities, and water and power departments

Municipal notes – Short term municipal bonds with maturities ranging from one day to five years

Mutual Fund – An investment company that owns a diverse group of bonds that is purchased and redeemed based on the fund's net asset value. The fund continues to issue new shares and redeem existing shares.

Original-issue discount bonds - Municipal bonds that were issued on their original offering below face value giving the bonds a special Federal tax benefit on the gain between face value and cost

Par – 100% of face value

Premium – A bond selling at a premium is selling above par or face value

Pre-Refunded Bonds – Bonds which have been refinanced, the proceeds of the refinance being held in escrow in U.S. government securities, until the call rate on the bonds

Standard & Poor's – A rating agency of municipal

bonds, corporate bonds, stocks and other investments

Yield to first call – The yield based on the current income plus taking into account the premium or discount to the call price

Yield to maturity – The yield based on the current income plus taking into account the premium or discount to face value as the bond approaches maturity

Zero coupon bonds - bonds that don't pay any current income, but are issued at a huge discount to par

ABOUT THE AUTHOR

Fred Fuld III was a former executive in the financial services industry who started out working as a stockbroker specializing in municipal bonds, and later as a market maker on the options floor of the Pacific Stock Exchange. He then became vice president of a San Francisco based investment management firm. He also worked as an adjunct professor for the College of Business of a California State University.

While working as a stockbroker, he started collecting antique stock certificates and other financial service industry collectibles. He then began selling antique stock and bond certificates through his firm, Investment Research Institute, and later, antiquestocks.com.

He is the publisher of WallStreetNewsNetwork.com, and has written numerous articles for various publications, including Friends of Financial History Magazine, the Bond and Share Society Journal, and Scripophily Magazine, and online websites such as TheStreet.com and Stockpickr.com. Television appearances include CNBC, Fox Business News, and Globo TV.

Other books by Fred Fuld III

Investment Trivia

Real Estate Trivia

Stock Market Trivia

Stock Market Trivia Volume 2

Buying Dividends: Revised and Updated: High Returns from the Dividend Capture System